SIMPLY SCIENCE

Weather

by Alice K. Flanagan

Content Adviser: Terrence E. Young Jr., M.Ed., M.L.S.,
Jefferson Parish (La.) Public Schools

Reading Adviser: Dr. Linda D. Labbo,
Department of Reading Education, College of Education,
The University of Georgia

 COMPASS POINT BOOKS

Minneapolis, Minnesota

Compass Point Books
3722 West 50th Street, #115
Minneapolis, MN 55410

Visit Compass Point Books on the Internet at *www.compasspointbooks.com* or e-mail your
request to *custserv@compasspointbooks.com*

Photographs ©:

Wm. L. Wantland/Tom Stack & Associates, cover; Visuals Unlimited/John Sohlden, 4; Photo Network/Tom Tracy, 5; Marilyn
Moseley LaMantia, 7; Greg Vaughn/Tom Stack and Associates, 9; Unicorn Stock Photos/Marcia Pennington, 10; Marilyn Moseley
LaMantia, 11; Visuals Unlimited/Frank Awbrey, 12; Sharon Gerig/Tom Stack and Associates, 13; Ed Darack/Colephoto, 15;
International Stock/Warren Faidley, 16; International Stock/Chad Ehlers, 17; Visuals Unlimited/William J. Weber, 18; Mark Allen
Stack/Tom Stack and Associates, 19; Sharon Gerig/Tom Stack and Associates, 20; Index Stock Imagery, 21; Visuals Unlimited/
John Sohlden, 22; Robin Cole/Colephoto, 23; Visuals Unlimited/Richard C. Walters, 24 top; Thomas Kitchin/Tom Stack and
Associates, 24 bottom; Visuals Unlimited/Mark A. Schneider, 25; Tsado/NCDC/NOAA/Tom Stack and Associates, 26; Therisa
Stack/Tom Stack and Associates, 27 top; International Stock/Warren Faidley, 27 bottom; Merrilee Thomas/Tom Stack and
Associates, 28.

Editors: E. Russell Primm, Emily J. Dolbear, and Melissa Stewart
Photo Researcher: Svetlana Zhurkina
Photo Selector: Dawn Friedman
Design: Bradfordesign, Inc.

Library of Congress Cataloging-in-Publication Data

Flanagan, Alice K.
  Weather / by Alice K. Flanagan.
    p. cm. — (Simply science)
  Includes bibliographical references (p.   ) and index.
  Summary: An introduction to some of the elements that make up our weather: sun, wind, clouds
and rain, and hurricanes and tornadoes.
  ISBN 0-7565-0039-7 (hardcover : lib. bdg.)
    1. Weather—Juvenile literature. [1. Weather.] I. Title. II. Simply science (Minneapolis, Minn.)
QC981.3 .F48 2000
  551.6—dc21   00-008562

Table of Contents

The Weather Today

Look outside today. Is it sunny, rainy, hot, or cold? Is it cloudy or clear? Is it calm or windy? All these things make up weather.

A sunny day on the beach

You need a raincoat on a rainy day.

Hot or Cold?

One of the most important things we want to know about the weather is the **air temperature**. Is it hot outside or cold?

In North America, it is usually hot in the summer and cold in the winter. To find out why, look at a globe that shows how Earth is shaped. Earth is round, like a ball. The Sun's hot rays cannot shine on every part of Earth at the same time.

Some parts of the world get very strong rays of sunlight every day. Other parts of the world get strong rays of sunlight for only part of the year.

Because Earth is round, different parts get different amounts of the sun's rays. ▶

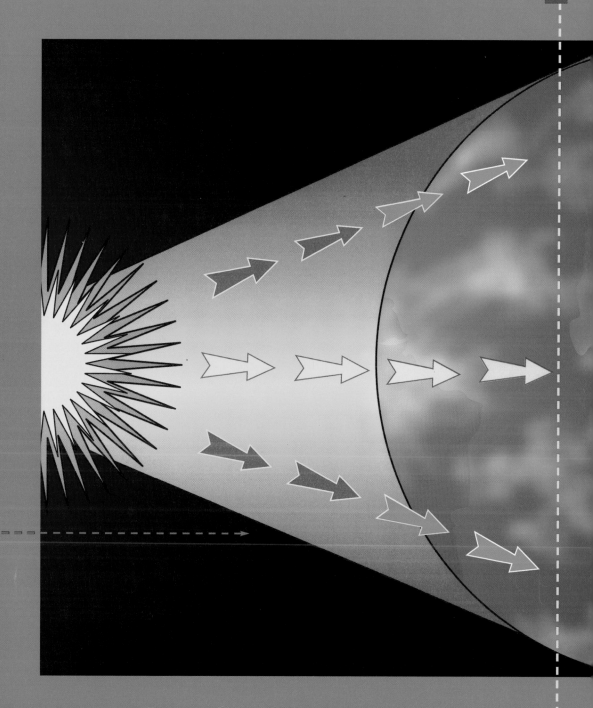

The **equator** is an **imaginary** line around the middle of Earth.

The parts of the world that are near the equator are always the hottest. They get strong rays of sunlight every day.

The parts of the world near the North and South Poles are always the coldest. Areas north of the equator get the strongest rays of sunlight in June, July, and August. Areas south of the equator get strong sunlight in December, January, and February.

We call the months when we get strong sunlight "summer." The time of year when we get the weakest sunlight is called "winter."

Windy or Calm?

Sunlight makes the air hot or cold. It also makes the air windy or calm.

Every day the Sun heats up some parts of the world more than others. The air above the hot places warms up too. The air above cold places stays cool.

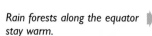

Rain forests along the equator stay warm.

Have you ever noticed that the upstairs part of a house is warmer in winter than the downstairs part? That is because warm air is lighter than cool air. Warm air rises, and cool air sinks.

The same thing happens to the air above Earth, but there is a lot more air up there. As the cold air sinks, it presses down on the warm air and makes it move. The moving air is called "wind."

Strong winds blowing a tree

Sinking cold air presses down on rising warm air to make wind.

Cold Air

Warm Air

Wind

What Changes Weather?

The cold air from the North and South Poles blows toward the equator. At the same time, warm air from the equator blows toward the poles. When the cold

Cold air blows up from the South Pole in Antarctica.

A cloud shaped by a mountain ▶

air and the warm air meet, it brings a change in the weather.

Mountains can also make weather change. High mountains stand in the way of blowing wind and moving clouds. That is why it is often rainy on one side of a mountain and dry on the other side.

Look at a map that shows how much rain falls in different places. Can you see the difference that high mountains make?

A storm in the mountains ▶

Where Do Clouds Come From?

Winds blow freely over the ocean because there is nothing to stop them. As the Sun heats the water, some of the water changes from a liquid into a gas. This water vapor rises into the air.

When water vapor touches a piece of dust in the air, it forms a tiny water droplet. Clouds are made up of these tiny water droplets and ice crystals.

An ocean storm

A lighthouse shows the way to shore for ships at sea.

Clouds come in many colors, shapes, and sizes. There are three main shapes: cumulus, stratus, and cirrus. **Cumulus clouds** look like puffy balls of cotton. They are low clouds. You can see them on a sunny summer day.

Cumulus clouds sometimes build up and turn into storm clouds. These clouds often bring rain showers. Sometimes they even bring thunder and lightning.

 Cumulous clouds

Cumulous clouds building into storm clouds

Cirrus clouds are thin and high. They look like feathers. Cirrus clouds are so thin that you can see blue skies or bright stars through them.

Stratus clouds are flat and low. You can see them on a gray day. Some stratus clouds form near the ground. They are called ground fog. Dark stratus clouds usually bring rain.

◄ Cirrus clouds

Stratus clouds ▶

Rain or Snow?

Rain comes from clouds. In warm parts of the world, the air is full of tiny water droplets. All the droplets in a cloud join together to form larger drops. When a great many droplets join together, the drop becomes heavy and falls to Earth as rain. Many droplets falling at once cause a hard rain.

Stratus clouds bringing rain

Rain drops splash on the ground.

◄ *Snowflakes have six sides.*

In cool parts of the world, the water droplets in a cloud freeze. They turn into ice and snow and fall to Earth. If the air temperature stays below 39° Fahrenheit (4° Celsius), snow will cover the ground. But if the ice runs into warmer air, it will melt and turn into rain.

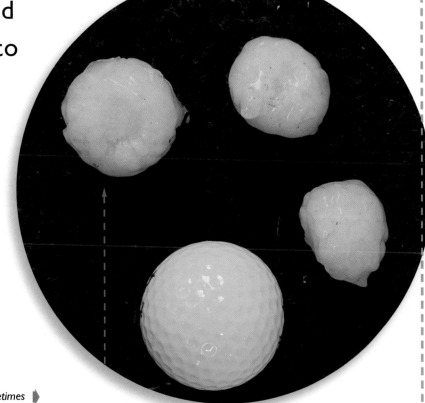

◀ *A winter storm*

Hailstones are sometimes ▶
as large as a golf ball.

Hurricanes and Tornadoes

Storms over oceans are called **hurricanes**. They begin when warm, wet air meets cold air. Clouds form and winds build up. If the storm grows in size, it may become a hurricane. Hurricanes spin very fast over the water. If they move onto land, the winds can destroy everything in

A hurricane viewed from space

Thunderstorms that cause tornadoes as seen from space

Houses destroyed by a hurricane

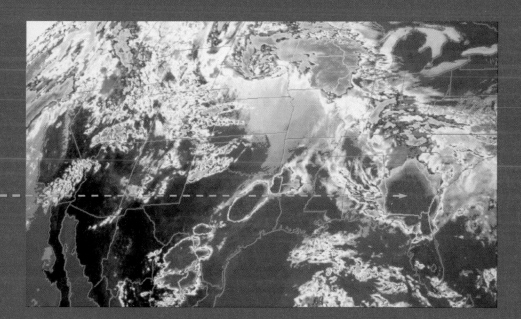

the storm's path. The rain caused by the hurricane can flood towns and kill many people.

Tornadoes begin like hurricanes, when warm, wet air meets cold air. But tornadoes form over land. The states of Nebraska, Kansas, and Oklahoma have a lot of tornadoes. Warm, damp air from the Gulf of Mexico often meets cold air coming from the Rocky Mountains.

The uneven air temperature creates a spinning cloud. A tornado cloud looks like a funnel. It moves at great speed across the flat land. It sucks things up like a giant vacuum cleaner.

◀ *A tornado*

Glossary

air temperature—a measurement of the amount of heat in the air

cirrus clouds—high, thin clouds

cumulus clouds—low, puffy clouds

equator—an imaginary line around the middle of the Earth

hurricane—a windy, spiraling storm that forms over the ocean

imaginary—not real

stratus clouds—low, flat clouds

tornado—a windy, whirling cloud shaped like a funnel. Tornadoes form over land.

Did You Know?

- Scientists who study the weather are called meteorologists.

- Every year, the United States is hit by about 1,200 tornadoes.

- Between 25 and 125 people die in these twisters each year.

- To be called a hurricane, a storm must have winds of at least 75 miles (120 kilometers) per hour.

- A cloud that causes a thunderstorm may be more than 4 miles (6 kilometers) high.

Want to Know More?

At the Library

Baxter, Nicola. *Rain, Wind, and Storm*. Austin, Tex.: Raintree Steck-Vaughn, 1998.

Herman, Gail. *Storm Chasers: Tracking Twisters*. New York: Grossett & Dunlap, 1997.

Kahl, Jonathan D. *Weather Watch: Forecasting the Weather*. Minneapolis: Lerner, 1996.

On the Web

National Weather Service

http://www.nws.noaa.gov/

For details about the weather for tomorrow and the next few days

Weather

http://weather.apoke.com/index.html

For information about storms, clouds, volcanoes, drought, flood, and other natural events

Through the Mail

Farmers' Almanac Order Desk

P.O. Box 1609

Mt. Hope Avenue

Lewiston, ME 04241

For long-range weather forecasts for an entire year

On the Road

Family Museum of Arts and Science

2900 Learning Campus Drive

Bettendorf, IA 52722

319/344-4106

To touch a tornado, make a cloud, and much more

Index

About the Author

Alice K. Flanagan writes books for children and teachers. Ever since she was a young girl, she has enjoyed writing. She has written more than seventy books on a wide variety of topics. Some of her books include biographies of U.S. presidents and their wives, biographies of people working in our neighborhoods, phonics books for beginning readers, and informational books about birds and Native Americans. Alice K. Flanagan lives in Chicago, Illinois.